PIANO | VOCAL | GUITAR

THE
ANDREW LLOYD WEBBER™
SHEET MUSIC COLLECTION

D1217746

Andrew Lloyd Webber™ is a trademark owned by Andrew Lloyd Webber.

ISBN 978-1-4950-9837-6

HAL•LEONARD®
7777 W. BLUEMOUND RD. P.O. BOX 13819 MILWAUKEE, WI 53213

In Australia Contact:
Hal Leonard Australia Pty. Ltd.
4 Lentara Court
Cheltenham, Victoria, 3192 Australia
Email: ausadmin@halleonard.com.au

Visit Hal Leonard Online at
www.halleonard.com

CONTENTS

4   ALL I ASK OF YOU...The Phantom of the Opera

16   AMIGOS PARA SIEMPRE (Friends for Life)...................Theme of the Barcelona 1992 Games

9   ANY DREAM WILL DO ....Joseph and the Amazing Technicolor® Dreamcoat

22   AS IF WE NEVER SAID GOODBYE..Sunset Boulevard

31   CLOSE EVERY DOOR............................Joseph and the Amazing Technicolor® Dreamcoat

38   DON'T CRY FOR ME ARGENTINA..Evita

46   EVERYTHING'S ALRIGHT..Jesus Christ Superstar

52   I BELIEVE MY HEART...The Woman in White

64   I DON'T KNOW HOW TO LOVE HIM ....Jesus Christ Superstar

59   I'M HOPELESS WHEN IT COMES TO YOU.............................Stephen Ward

68   LOVE CHANGES EVERYTHING.......................................Aspects of Love

80   LOVE NEVER DIES ....Love Never Dies

73   MEMORY..Cats

88   THE MUSIC OF THE NIGHT ....The Phantom of the Opera

94   NO MATTER WHAT..Whistle Down the Wind

104   THE PERFECT YEAR ....Sunset Boulevard

110   THE PHANTOM OF THE OPERA............................The Phantom of the Opera

99   PIE JESU..Requiem

118   STICK IT TO THE MAN ....School of Rock

124   SUPERSTAR ....Jesus Christ Superstar

130   TELL ME ON A SUNDAY ....Song & Dance

135   'TIL I HEAR YOU SING..Love Never Dies

140   WHISTLE DOWN THE WIND ....Whistle Down the Wind

156   YOU MUST LOVE ME...Evita

144   YOU'RE IN THE BAND..School of Rock

ALL I ASK OF YOU
from THE PHANTOM OF THE OPERA

Music by ANDREW LLOYD WEBBER
Lyrics by CHARLES HART
Additional Lyrics by RICHARD STILGOE

ANY DREAM WILL DO

from JOSEPH AND THE AMAZING TECHNICOLOR® DREAMCOAT

Music by ANDREW LLOYD WEBBER
Lyrics by TIM RICE

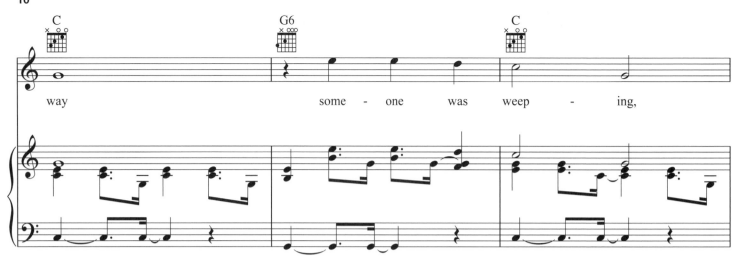

way ... some - one was weep - ing,

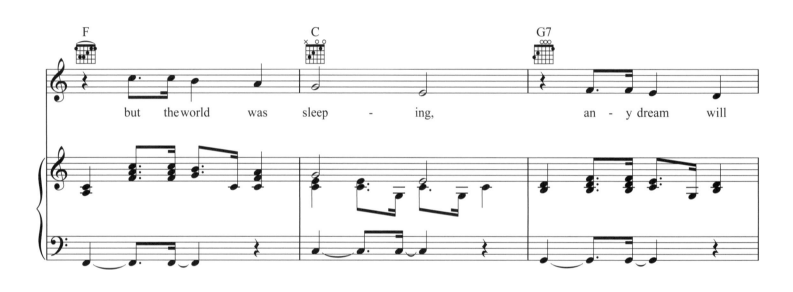

but the world was sleep - ing, an - y dream will

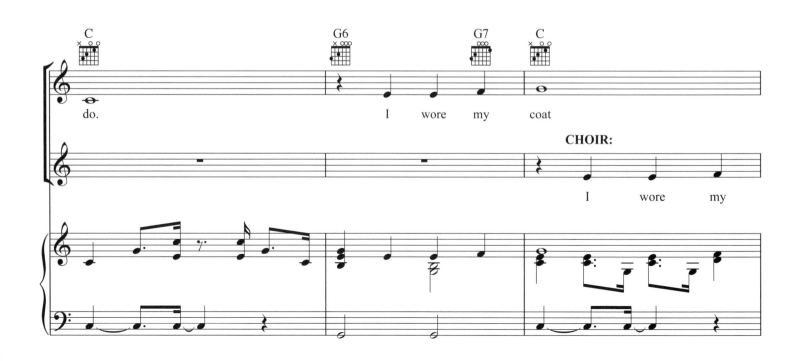

do. ... I wore my coat

CHOIR:

I wore my

AMIGOS PARA SIEMPRE
(Friends for Life)
(The Official Theme of the Barcelona 1992 Games)

Music by ANDREW LLOYD WEBBER
Lyrics by DON BLACK

Gentle Habanera feel
F
B♭m6/F
F
mf
B♭m6/F
F
I ___ don't have to say a word to you, ___ you seem to know what - ev - er
We ___ share mem - o - ries I won't for - get. ___ And we'll share more, my friend, we
Gm/F
B♭m/F
F
mood I'm go - ing through. Feel as though I've known you for - ev - er.
have - n't start - ed yet. Some - thing hap - pens when we're to - geth - er.

AS IF WE NEVER SAID GOODBYE

from SUNSET BOULEVARD

Music by ANDREW LLOYD WEBBER
Lyrics by DON BLACK & CHRISTOPHER HAMPTON,
with contributions by AMY POWERS

CLOSE EVERY DOOR

from JOSEPH AND THE AMAZING TECHNICOLOR® DREAMCOAT

Music by ANDREW LLOYD WEBBER
Lyrics by TIM RICE

DON'T CRY FOR ME ARGENTINA

from EVITA

Words by TIM RICE
Music by ANDREW LLOYD WEBBER

look at me to know that ev-'ry word is true. __

EVERYTHING'S ALRIGHT

from JESUS CHRIST SUPERSTAR

Words by TIM RICE
Music by ANDREW LLOYD WEBBER

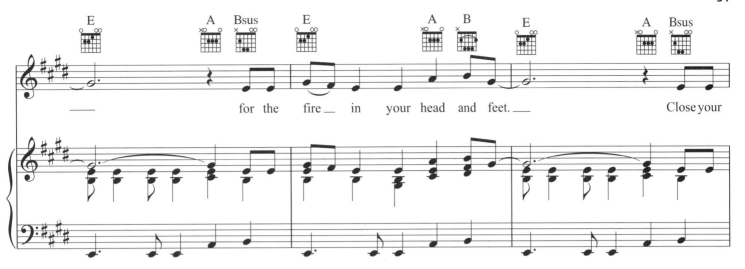

for the fire __ in your head and feet. __ Close your

eyes,   close your eyes and re - lax, think of noth - ing to - night. _____

APOSTLES' WOMEN: Close your   eyes,   close your eyes and re -

Hard Rock (♩♩ = ♩♩)

*Repeat many times, crescendo to **f**, then fade*

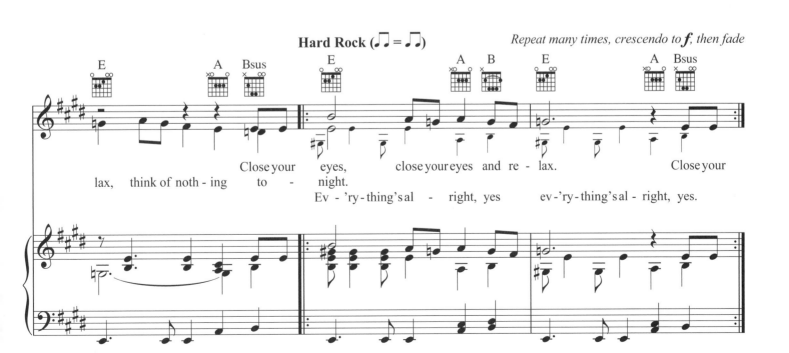

lax,   think of noth - ing to - night.

Close your   eyes,   close your eyes and re - lax.   Close your

Ev - 'ry - thing's al - right, yes   ev - 'ry - thing's al - right, yes.

I BELIEVE MY HEART

from THE WOMAN IN WHITE

Music by ANDREW LLOYD WEBBER
Lyrics by DAVID ZIPPEL

HARTRIGHT:
When-ev-er I look at you, — the world dis-ap-pears. All in a sin-gle glance so re-veal-ing. —

I'M HOPELESS WHEN IT COMES TO YOU

from STEPHEN WARD

Music by ANDREW LLOYD WEBBER
Book and Lyrics by DON BLACK
and CHRISTOPHER HAMPTON

feel - ings. I'm hope-less when it comes to you. You're

bruised but you're not bro - ken, there'll be no more lies.

We'll go on to-geth - er, dry each oth - er's eyes. This will

make us strong-er than be - fore. Some-times that's what pain can

I DON'T KNOW HOW TO LOVE HIM

from JESUS CHRIST SUPERSTAR

Words by TIM RICE
Music by ANDREW LLOYD WEBBER

LOVE CHANGES EVERYTHING
from ASPECTS OF LOVE

Music by ANDREW LLOYD WEBBER
Lyrics by DON BLACK and CHARLES HART

Drammatico

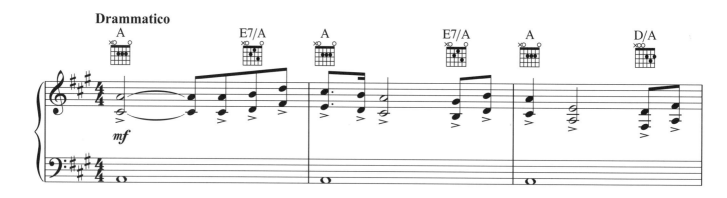

Love,   love chang - es ev - 'ry - thing: hands and
Love,   love chang - es ev - 'ry - thing: days are

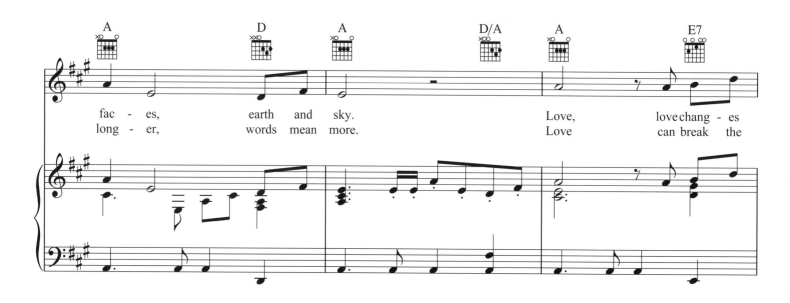

fac - es,   earth and sky.   Love,   love chang - es
long - er,   words mean more.   Love   can break the

MEMORY
from CATS

Music by ANDREW LLOYD WEBBER
Text by TREVOR NUNN after T.S. ELIOT

Mid - night. _____ Not a sound from the pave - ment. _____ Has the moon lost her
Mem - ory _____ all a - lone in the moon - light _____ I can smile at the

mem - ory? _____ She is smil - ing a - lone. _____ In the
old days, _____ I was beau - ti - ful then. _____ I re -

lamp - light the with-ered leaves col - lect at my feet _____ and the
mem - ber the time I knew what hap-pi-ness was, _____ let the

wind _____ be - gins to moan.

mem - ory live a - gain.

Ev - 'ry street lamp seems to beat _____ a

Burnt out ends of smo - ky days, ____ the stale cold smell ____ of

Db

morn - ing. _____ The street lamp dies, an - oth - er

Bbm7　　**Ebm7**

Ab7　　**Dbmaj7**　　**Bbm**　　**Eb7**

night is o - ver, ___ an - oth - er day is

Ab　　**Ab7**　　**Db**

dawn - ing. Touch me. _____ It's so eas - y to

rit.　　*a tempo*

Bbm　　**Gb**

leave me _____ all a - lone with the mem - ory _____ of my days in the

rall.

LOVE NEVER DIES
from LOVE NEVER DIES

Music by ANDREW LLOYD WEBBER
Lyrics by GLENN SLATER

Who

rall.

THE MUSIC OF THE NIGHT
from THE PHANTOM OF THE OPERA

Music by ANDREW LLOYD WEBBER
Lyrics by CHARLES HART
Additional Lyrics by RICHARD STILGOE

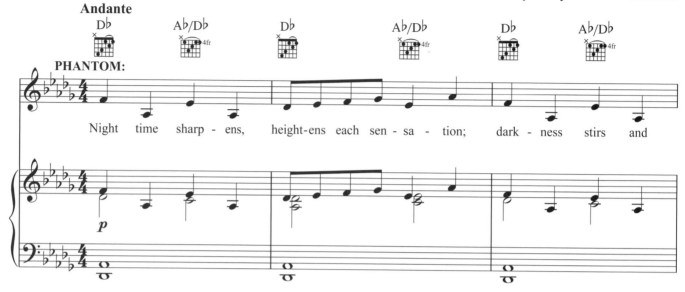

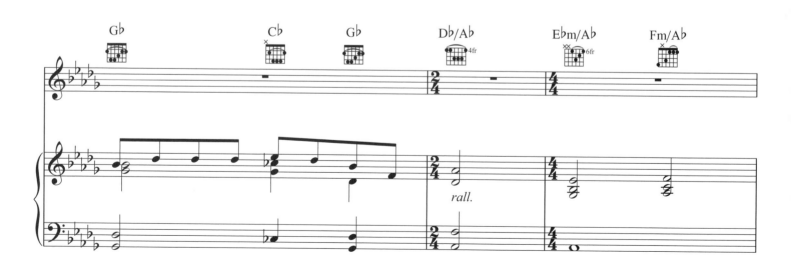

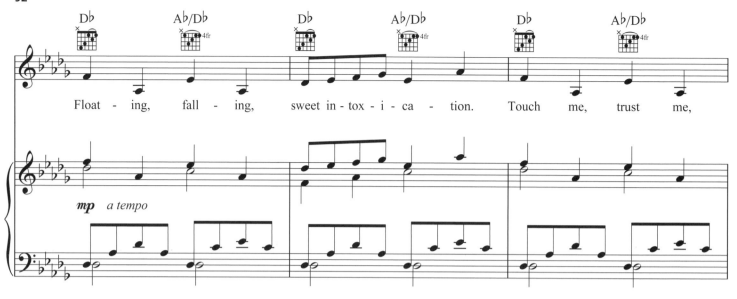

Float - ing, fall - ing, sweet in - tox - i - ca - tion. Touch me, trust me,

sa - vour each sen - sa - tion. Let the dream be - gin, let your dark - er side give in to the

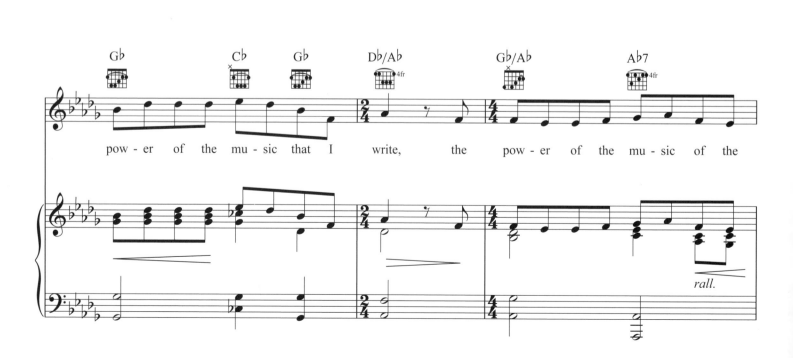

pow - er of the mu - sic that I write, the pow - er of the mu - sic of the

NO MATTER WHAT
from WHISTLE DOWN THE WIND

Music by ANDREW LLOYD WEBBER
Lyrics by JIM STEINMAN

No mat-ter what they tell us, no mat-ter what they do,
If on-ly tears were laugh-ter, if on-ly night was day,

no mat-ter what they teach us, what we be-lieve is true.
if on-ly prayers were an-swered, then we would hear God say:

I know our love's for - ev - er,
No mat - ter where it's bar - ren,

I know no mat - ter what.
our dream is be - ing born.

PIE JESU
from REQUIEM

By ANDREW LLOYD WEBBER

re - qui - em.

SOLO BOY: *mp*

Pi - e Je - su, ____ pi - e Je - su, ____ pi - e

Je - su, ____ pi - e Je - su, Qui tol - lis pec - ca - ta mun - di,

Qui tol - lis pec - ca - ta mun - di,

SOPRANO

ALTO

Hm ____

TENOR

BASS

THE PERFECT YEAR
from SUNSET BOULEVARD

Music by ANDREW LLOYD WEBBER
Lyrics by DON BLACK and CHRISTOPHER HAMPTON

ball - room,　ev - 'ry - thing I want is here,　if you're with

me, _____ next year will be _____ the per - fect year. **JOE:** Be - fore we

play _____ some dan - ger - ous game, _____ be - fore we fan _____ some harm - less

flame, _____ we have to ask _____ if this is wise, _____ and if the

THE PHANTOM OF THE OPERA

from THE PHANTOM OF THE OPERA

Music by ANDREW LLOYD WEBBER
Lyrics by CHARLES HART
Additional Lyrics by RICHARD STILGOE and MIKE BATT

CHRISTINE: In sleep he sang to me, _____ in dreams he came,

STICK IT TO THE MAN
from SCHOOL OF ROCK

Music by ANDREW LLOYD WEBBER
Lyrics by GLENN SLATER

SUPERSTAR
from JESUS CHRIST SUPERSTAR

Words by TIM RICE
Music by ANDREW LLOYD WEBBER

TELL ME ON A SUNDAY

from SONG & DANCE

Music by ANDREW LLOYD WEBBER
Lyrics by DON BLACK

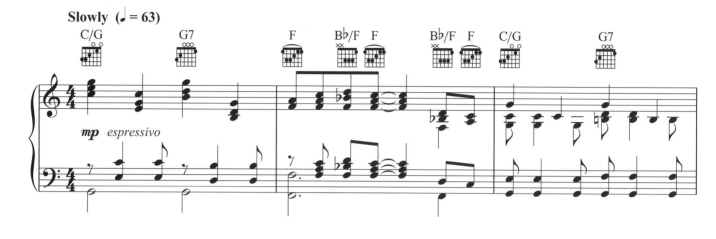

Don't write a let-ter when you want to leave,

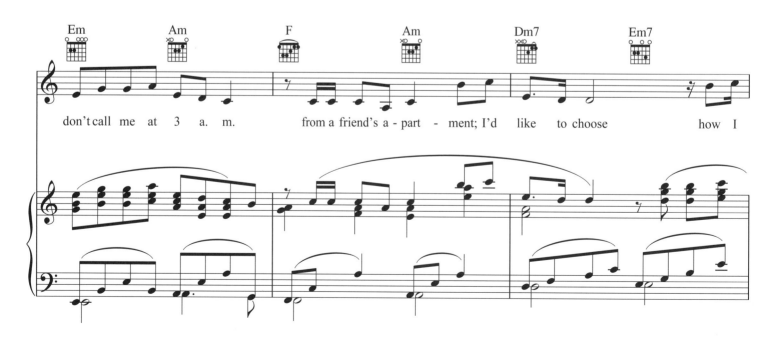

don't call me at 3 a.m. from a friend's a-part-ment; I'd like to choose how I

'Til I Hear You Sing

from LOVE NEVER DIES

Music by ANDREW LLOYD WEBBER
Lyrics by GLENN SLATER

The day starts. The day ends. Time crawls by.

Night steals in, pac-ing the floor. The mo-ments

creep, yet I can't bear to sleep 'Til I hear you sing... And

WHISTLE DOWN THE WIND
from WHISTLE DOWN THE WIND

Music by ANDREW LLOYD WEBBER
Lyrics by JIM STEINMAN

YOU'RE IN THE BAND

from SCHOOL OF ROCK

Music by ANDREW LLOYD WEBBER
Lyrics by GLENN SLATER

DEWEY: *Ever play the electric guitar?*
ZACK: *My dad says it's a waste of time.*
DEWEY: *Oh yeah? Well let's waste time together, shall we?*

Driving Rock groove

DEWEY:

Grab a hold of your axe ___ and try to pluck out this riff. ___

[DEWEY plucks out a riff on the guitar. ZACK dutifully imitates him.]

Good! Let your shoul-ders re- lax, ___ you don't wan-na be so stiff. ___

Keep on rock-in' each note, grab it right by the throat. Keep the rhy-thm a-float, don't for-get to e-mote! And that's all that she wrote. Ba-by, you're in the band!

[Next, he turns to LAWRENCE.]
DEWEY: *Piano man!*
LAWRENCE: *Lawrence.*
DEWEY: *Whatever, dude, come here!*

If you

SUMMER: *Manager?* DEWEY:

how a-bout _ be-ing man-a-ger? Is that some-thing you could swing? _

SUMMER: *What does it mean?*

DEWEY:

— It means I'm put-ting YOU _ in charge of the

SUMMER: *(Pumping fist)* DEWEY:

whole damn thing! Yes! We've got our band! _

[All instruments drop out except the drums, played by FREDDIE.]

N.C.

DEWEY *(2nd time)*: Now, Freddie, keep that
beat going. Katie, come in on G...

Drums only

Bass (last time only)

DEWEY (*2nd time*)**:** *Just give me that G, lay it down there. Zack, hit me with some big fat chords.*

DEWEY (*2nd time*)**:** *Awesome! Lawrence, take me to the moon!*

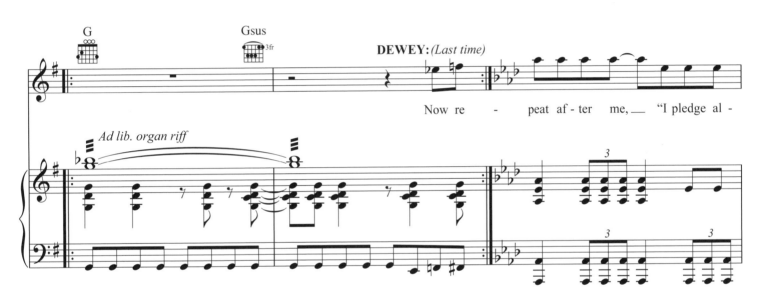

DEWEY: (*Last time*)

Now re - peat af - ter me, __ "I pledge al -

Ad lib. organ riff

le - giance to the band." __

"And I

KIDS:

"I pledge al - le - giance to the band." __

YOU MUST LOVE ME

from the Cinergi Motion Picture EVITA

Words by TIM RICE
Music by ANDREW LLOYD WEBBER

Flowing

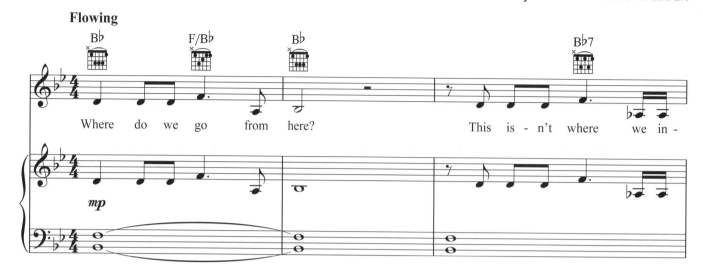

Where do we go from here? This is-n't where we in-

tend-ed to be. We had it all, you be-lieved in me, I be-

lieved in you. Cer-tain-ties
Why are you
dis-ap-
at my